KIDS FIGHT EXTINCTION

MARTIN DOREY

ILLUSTRATED BY TIM WESSON

WALKER
BOOKS

CONTENTS

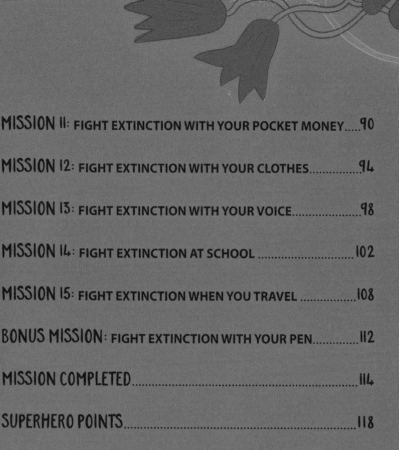

ARE YOU
READY TO BE
A SUPERHERO?

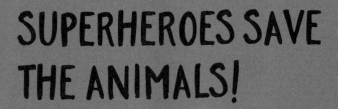

SUPERHEROES SAVE THE ANIMALS!

Are you ready to save animals and be a #2minutesuperhero? Of course you are!

Right. What can you do in 2 minutes? Tidy your room? Maybe. Drink a can of pop? Probably. Brush your teeth? Just. Save animals from extinction? Definitely.

2 minutes is all you need to do something amazing, such as...

Giving nature a hand.

Changing your habits.

Saving the planet.

NATURE NEEDS YOU

Our planet is facing a crisis. Lots of plants, animals, mammals and insects are facing extinction. That means they will die out if we don't help them. Once they are gone they will be gone for ever.

It's going to take some pretty special – but very normal – people to fight extinction and help save nature.

That's YOU.

Why you? Because, believe it or not, you have the power to make a difference. You don't need a cape or a mask or to be able to fly or fight baddies in the intergalactic wotsit to help solve the crisis. You just have to be you.

Because you've got what it takes.

This book will show you how, in just a few minutes, you can help to fight extinction, help restore nature, take care of animals and plants and save the planet. And – while doing it – become a #2minutesuperhero.

Not a bad trade-off, right?

Ready to save me and be a superhero?

WHY YOU ARE THE IDEAL #2MINUTESUPERHERO

You have the power to help fight extinction, from your brilliant brain to your superhero smile. The most important thing to remember is: everything you do makes a difference in helping to save the planet, no matter how small.

EYES: Help you to see the changes you are making! Go you!

BRAIN: Your greatest weapon!!! Thinking about how to solve problems is a true superpower.

MOUTH: To shout for all the plants and animals that don't have a voice.

EARS: Are made for listening to help you find out what you can do!

SMILE:
To make saving the planet more fun!

HEART:
Big-hearted superheroes make the best planet-savers because they LOVE nature.

LEGS:
Are made for walking, right? To help you in your missions.

ARMS:
For taking care of the practical stuff, such as tree planting and doing the thumbs up.

WHEELS:
Transport for you to spread the message, "Save the Planet!"

SOMETHING TO REMEMBER

There will be times when it'll be easy to see the results of your actions. There may be other times when you won't see the effects of your hard work. In these times it's important to remember that everything you do matters and will have some kind of effect, in some way, at some point, somewhere in the world.

ME AND MY #2MINUTEMISSION

Before we get started, I would like to tell you a bit about myself. My name is Martin. I am an eco-activist, beach cleaner and writer. Many years ago I started picking up litter on my local beach. I started putting pictures of that litter on social media, using a new hashtag **#2minutebeachclean**. Lots of people joined in and before I knew it the whole thing went global!!!

Now, the organization I started is a charity that aims to save the planet 2 minutes at a time. The experience made me believe that anyone can make a difference and that everyone has the power to change the world through small actions. Why? Because lots of small actions add up to make a BIG difference.

You can be a **#2minutesuperhero**. If you make small changes in your life, you could be making life better for an animal, insect or bird somewhere. You might never see it. But it does matter!

EVERYDAY SUPERHERO

Name: Martin

Job: Writer

Superpower: Using words to get people to do good stuff

How you fight extinction: I pick up litter, write books, plant trees and ride my bike

Top tip: Everybody can make a difference

Hates: Wasting energy

Loves: Solar showers

MARTIN

YOUR EXTINCTION ARMOURY

Fighting extinction isn't going to be easy. But you have a huge armoury of "weapons" and actions you can use to help you. When a superhero uses them wisely – and we'll find out how later – they make you invincible (or very difficult to argue with, which is just as good IMHO).

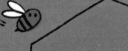

MAKING THINGS:
There are lots of exciting things you can do to help nature, such as building hedgehog houses or bee hotels.

GETTING ARTY:
Do you like painting, drawing, playing music or acting? Great!!! You can change the world with a song, a picture or even a piece of theatre.

CHANGING THE WAY YOU DO THINGS:
Sometimes just a little change can make all the difference, even though you may never see it.

GOING WITHOUT STUFF:
You might have to do without some things, such as fish or meat, to make a difference.

WRITING LETTERS:
Letters, when supercharged with powerful facts, armour-piercing ideas and explosive arguments can make more of a difference than any army could.

THE MEDIA:

Newspapers, Internet sites and TV channels can be really powerful. The media can help you share your story with other superheroes in the making.

GOING ONLINE:

Ideas can travel round the world super fast online. If it's safe, and if your parents or carers let you, going online can be another powerful weapon.

BUYING THINGS (OR NOT BUYING THEM):

Companies that are harming nature don't deserve your pocket money. Spend it on the good guys instead!

TALKING:

Chatting with your friends is a great way to change things. The more people on your side, the more people will listen.

MAKING POSTERS AND PLACARDS:

Share your message and make people take notice. Put posters and placards in your window at home or in school.

PROTESTING:

As long as you do it legally and peacefully, protesting can be a great way of making your voice heard. Attending a rally, where people come together in a group, or even sitting outside your school like Greta Thunberg is a form of protest. You could organize your own or join one (with your parents or carers).

HOW TO USE THIS BOOK

♠ This book contains a series of **MISSIONS**. Each will help you to understand extinction and the natural world and how we fit into it. Crucially, each mission explains what you can do to fight it and the areas of your life where you **CAN** make a difference.

♠ The big missions all contain **2 MINUTE MISSIONS**.

♠ These are tasks that I want you to do. Each task is worth superhero points and will require you to use something in your armoury.

♠ Some of the **2 MINUTE MISSIONS** are hard. Some are easy. The harder missions will earn you more points. Some will also take longer than 2 minutes!

♠ After you complete a mission, count up the points you have earned and make a note of them.

♠ Once you have finished the book, add up your points to get your final score. Turn to page 124 and find out what kind of superhero you are.

ARE YOU READY?

Sign here. Before you start, I need to know that you are committed to saving nature. Will you take the pledge?

I solemnly pledge my allegiance to nature.

I will fight extinction through my actions and will take **2** minutes of every day to help nature, the natural world and the animals who share our planet.

Training approved by:

Founder of the #2minutebeachclean

YOUR MISSIONS START NOW...

GET TO KNOW EXTINCTION

Welcome to the training school for superheroes!

It's like a school but not like a school. For a start it's got animals, plants and even a dinosaur. And there are no desks or lessons, just a lot of fun stuff to do and missions to complete.

At Superhero School you will learn all about extinction, why it's important to fight it and why fighting for one animal means you fight for all animals.

It's not easy to understand extinction in just a few lines. In fact, it's a bit complicated at times. But bear with it, because it will help you to understand why we need to act and how we can use our superhero powers (and by that I mean our eyes, ears and brains, wheels, hearts and voices) to start to fight extinction.

It's a great story and has sad bits and happy bits, and did I mention the dinosaurs?

Let's begin at the beginning.

WHAT IS EXTINCTION?

Extinction is the complete disappearance of a fish, bird, plant, mammal or reptile from Earth. It is what happens when the last of its kind (or species) dies.

Extinction is a natural process and has been happening since life on Earth began.

Think of the dinosaurs. They lived on Earth for about 175 million years and then became extinct after what scientists believe was a major event – an asteroid strike perhaps – around 65 million years ago. Most of them were wiped out, with the exception of those that went on to become birds. (It is amazing to think, isn't it, that the birds in your garden are descended from dinosaurs!)

INTERVIEW WITH A DINOSAUR

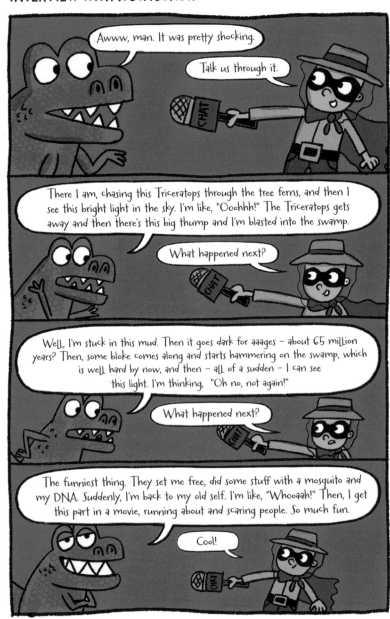

FOSSILY FASCINATING

What we know about dinosaurs comes from fossils, which are their preserved skeletons. Fossils are formed when an animal or plant dies and is covered in mud or ash, which then turns, over millions of years, into rock and stone.

There are lots of places where it is possible to find fossils where they have waited for you for millions of years, but you can also find them in surprising places too. You can see fossils everywhere, even in the stone used to make buildings on your high street.

YOUR 2 MINUTE MISSION: Use your superhero eyes to go on a fossil hunt! 10 POINTS

1. Visit your local museum.
2. Look for stone in your high street. Look at: www.londonpavementgeology.co.uk
3. If you can, get your family or carers to take you on a fossil hunt to an area that has lots.

IF EXTINCTION IS NATURAL, WHAT'S THE PROBLEM?

Before today there were five events that caused mass extinctions. This is when lots of the creatures on Earth died out. Some of these events caused as many as 90% of land animals to die off. One of these wiped out (almost) all the dinosaurs. Others wiped out plants and sea creatures. Some of these events were caused by massive catastrophes like asteroids or volcanic eruptions, but some happened over millions of years.

In "normal" times we would expect species to go extinct for all kinds of reasons, but what is happening now is that many more species are threatened with extinction than is normal. In fact, the rate of extinction, according to the World Wildlife Fund is about 1,000 times higher than it should be.

That's scary, huh?

YES. THEY ARE RELATED!!!!

Great, Great, Great, Great, Great, Great, Great Grandma!!!

WHY IS EXTINCTION BAD?

Aside from losing exciting – and scary – creatures like the Tyrannosaurus Rex, extinction is bad for all of us.

When an animal, like a tiger or rhinoceros, goes extinct it means that it is lost for ever. Obviously it's bad for that species, but it's also bad for the species that it shares a habitat with, that depend on it or that are controlled by it.

If we allow this to happen then all the ecosystems (these are like mini planets within a planet) that depend on those species will collapse, threatening the safety of our food, water and societies.

Lots of things cause extinctions. You can read about them later.

SCARY FACT: Between 1970 and 2014 the planet lost, on average, 60% of its populations of mammals, birds, fish, reptiles and amphibians.

WHY STOP THE EXTINCTIONS?

Planet Earth is beautiful. It is our home. It is also home to
millions of insects, birds, mammals, fish, reptiles and plants.
Each of us depends on the other for food, shelter, water and life.
It has a delicate balance that is at risk if thousands of species are
lost. Imagine a line of dominoes. When one falls, the rest go too.

Everything on Earth is related.

**HUMMINGBIRDS
LOVE NECTAR BECAUSE:**

It's their food! Hummingbirds have
evolved to be able to hover in front
of flowers and use their long beaks
to get access to the nectar, which is
right inside the flower.

FLOWERS LOVE HUMMINGBIRDS BECAUSE:
When the hummingbird visits flowers collecting nectar they also collect pollen on their feathers and take it to other plants, helping to fertilize the new plants and playing a vital part in producing new plants.

WITHOUT THE HUMMINGBIRDS:
The plants wouldn't be able to reproduce and so the plants would die.

WITHOUT THE PLANTS:
The hummingbirds would die because they would have no food.

IF YOU PROTECT:
The flowers you also protect the hummingbird.

27

EXTINCT VS FUNCTIONALLY EXTINCT

What's the difference? Functionally extinct is the way scientists describe types of animals that have so few members that they cannot recover.

Najin and Fatu are the last northern white rhinos. They are mother and daughter. There are no males left, which means that when Najin and Fatu die their kind will die. It is very sad.

It makes me cross, because the rest of their family was killed by poachers and war. But it also makes me determined because there are other animals that we can save. And that's why we need to step up and make a difference, no matter how small it is.

WHAT IS THE IUCN RED LIST?

This is a list of the most critically endangered animals, insects, birds and fish on Earth. There are about 138,300 species on the Red List. It is compiled by the International Union for Conservation of Nature, an organization made up of the cleverest scientists and a staff in over 50 countries. They provide facts and information on endangered animals so that governments act.

WHY DO WE NEED TO ACT NOW?

Today we are at a point in time when it's not too late to change. It's a really important moment for our planet. The United Nations has announced that around 1,000,000 species are at risk of extinction now. They haven't gone extinct yet. It's too late for the northern white rhino (I'm still a bit sad about that) but not for millions of other species. That means we still have a chance.

If we act decisively to save nature then we will all benefit. I'm sorry that it falls to your generation to do this important work when a lot of my generation stood around and let it happen.

But it's not all bad news. While we have a chance to change, we still have hope. And that's a reason to smile.

Now is the time to act. Shall we do it?

Yes!

THE CAUSES OF EXTINCTION

In any fight, whether it's for more space on the sofa or for free ice cream, it's important that you, as a superhero, understand what the battle is for, why it's important and, perhaps most importantly, what you can do about it.

What do we know? We know we are fighting for nature against extinction. But we also have to understand the causes of extinction in order to work out what we can do about it. Unless you can get to the root cause of the problem you are only really treating the effects of the problem.

In the case of extinction, sadly, one of the main causes is the effect we, as humans, have on our planet.

GREAT NEWS!!!
What this means is that everything you do that's kind to the planet will help in the fight against extinction.

We've already talked a little bit about historical extinctions, which were caused by events like asteroid strikes and changing climates. These are the kind of events that killed off the dinosaurs but that don't bother us today. Plus, we can't do anything about them, other than learn from the experience. Mind you, dinosaurs are cool, right?

But you might have heard scientists and newspapers talk about what is happening today as the "sixth mass extinction". There are lots of reasons why animals go extinct or are at risk of extinction. Some of these are caused by man while others are the result of the way things change over time. What's worrying, as I have said before, is the rate at which the extinctions and changes are happening today. Because of us humans.

❌ THE DEARLY DEPARTED ❌

Name: Steggy

Job: Stegosaurus

Superpower: Having a spiky tail to ward off predators

How extinction affects you: Sadly I went extinct, possibly because I was too stupid to compete with other dinosaurs

Top tip: Develop your brain instead of spikes if you want to survive

Hates: That he wasn't a bird

Loves: Eating small bushes

❌ STEGGY ❌

EXTINCTION BY NATURAL SELECTION

Lots of animals and plants have gone extinct during our planet's long history (4 and a half billon years, in case you were wondering) for lots of reasons. One of these is natural selection, an idea coined by Charles Darwin, to describe the natural way animals and plants evolve (and leave others behind).

WHY DOES IT CAUSE EXTINCTION?

Natural selection is when an animal dies out because it cannot compete anymore, can't adapt to changing climate, weather or environment (or just isn't very good at it).

YOUR IMPERFECT COUSIN

Did you know that there were lots of types of humans before us? Some of them were known as Neanderthals and they lived as recently as 35,000 years ago. They became extinct after they were outcompeted by modern humans (us). They had language, used tools, made fire and hunted but were pushed into extinction because modern humans had better tools, hunting techniques and ability to survive. They are often portrayed as stupid, but they weren't.

TODAY'S EXTINCTION THREATS

We can't do anything about past extinctions. But we may be able to do something about those that are about to happen.

Your next task then is to get to know WHY they are happening.

CHANGING CLIMATE AND WARMING SEAS

Climate change is having a huge effect on the natural world.
It affects everything, from the creatures at the bottom of the
ocean to insects and birds.

It's complicated, but it's about changing weather patterns
caused by the greenhouse effect of gases including carbon
dioxide and methane emitted by human activity. The gases are
causing the planet to warm up gradually, and this is causing the
seas to warm up and for weather patterns to change all across
the planet.

WHY IS IT CAUSING EXTINCTION?

Gases that are building in the atmosphere are causing the
temperature of the planet to warm up. It might be only a tiny
bit, but it affects all of us. Animals that have adapted to live
in specialized conditions are finding that their food is moving
away, that they cannot survive or that their homes are being
destroyed by fires or flooding.

HABITAT DESTRUCTION

If someone destroyed your home, how would you feel? Awful, right? That's exactly what is happening to lots of animals and plants all over the world. In fact, it's one of the most common reasons why animals are facing extinction. Humans are just too greedy and are taking up all the land for themselves!!!

The homes of animals and plants are being destroyed all over the world. Habitats are lost due to climate change, because of wildfires or flooding, or because jungle and woodland is being turned into farmland or to make cities and towns bigger.

WHY IS IT CAUSING EXTINCTION?

Some animals are so highly specialized that they can only live in one place. If that place gets destroyed they have nowhere to go, nothing to eat and no shelter.

HUMAN ENCROACHMENT

What would happen if your local council wanted to build a car park on your house? You wouldn't have anywhere to go! It's the same for animals whose lives have been disrupted by us. When humans take over the homes of animals or plants it leaves them nowhere else to go.

WHY IS IT CAUSING EXTINCTION?

As our cities expand and the land we use to grow food and live spreads out, we come into ever closer contact with animals and plants that were previously just our neighbours. Who do you think comes off worse when humans encroach on the natural world? Usually the animals, sadly.

DEFORESTATION

The forests are vital for the health of our planet because they provide a place for countless animals to live and also prevent flooding and erosion.

Trees provide a lot of the oxygen we need to breathe through photosynthesis. They also store carbon, which is important in the fight against climate change, and they help to reduce pollution in cities.

Basically, forests are amazing!!!

WHY IS IT CAUSING EXTINCTION?

Deforestation is devastating for the animals living in the forest. When forests and trees get cut down for timber or are destroyed to make room for farms and crops, this has a terrible effect on our ecosystems, threatening the lives of animals and living things all over the world.

HUMAN PREDATION AND POACHING

We've been eating and hunting animals for as long as we've been on the planet. Long ago we hunted for food or to defend ourselves from animals that scared us or were a threat to us, like lions, poisonous snakes and bears. We also hunted animals for their products, like fur from seals or ivory from elephants.

Poaching is when animals are killed illegally for their fur, tusks or skins. It is estimated that around 35,000 elephants are killed by poachers every year. Elephants, along with lions, zebra and rhinos are likely to go extinct in your lifetime unless we act.

WHY IS IT CAUSING EXTINCTION?

Sadly, throughout human history we have killed animals either for food, fur or fun. It's so terribly sad that so many animals have died out because we have been so greedy, stupid and cruel.

- 43% of the African lion population has disappeared in the last 21 years.

- There are only about 1,000 mountain gorillas left in Africa.

- It is said that the last wolf was shot in Britain in 1680.

- Some people think that brown bears went extinct in Britain as recently as 500AD.

- The great auk, a flightless seabird, was hunted to extinction for its fat and feathers by 1850.

KILLING FOR FUN

Hunting for sport is when people kill animals just because they can. Some people like to kill animals for their skins or to hang trophies of their heads on their wall.

Animals that are hunted for trophies are usually males that have big antlers, manes or horns. Killing them has a disastrous effect on populations as it wipes out the strongest males from the breeding stock, making them more vulnerable.

It is estimated that the African lion population has fallen by 30% and may now number as few as 39,000. And yet African lions may legally be hunted in Tanzania, Zimbabwe and Senegal.

SAD FACT: In the last 10 years, hunters have taken home over 1.7 million "trophies" from animals they have killed for "sport". More than 200,000 of them were from animals in danger of going extinct.

POLLUTION

Pollution can take many forms whether from plastic, acid rain, industry or agriculture. However it is always something – a chemical or physical body – that is toxic to the environment and upsets the natural balance of ecosystems threatening thousands of species around the world.

WHY IS IT CAUSING EXTINCTION?

Pollution, when it gets into contact with sensitive ecosystems, can cause damage to food, the air, water or the earth so that nothing can grow. In the case of plastic pollution it can also kill animals if they eat it or get tangled in it.

BAD NEWS!!!
The flesh footed shearwaters of Australia are endangered because of plastic. The adults feed at sea – picking up plastic instead of food – and feed it to their chicks at their nest sites. The chicks then die because they have full stomachs but no nutrition. Some colonies of the birds have declined by as much as 50% while other colonies have disappeared altogether.

PESTICIDES

Pesticides are chemicals or compounds that are used to kill insects or organisms that are harmful to cultivated plants in agriculture. While they stop pests from eating or destroying crops or causing harm to livestock, they can also cause terrible damage to ecosystems because they get ingested by worms, insects and other plants endangering the balance of nature.

WHY IS IT CAUSING EXTINCTION?

In the case of bees, pesticides are causing their numbers to decline rapidly because they either kill the bees when they land on flowers or they kill the colony when the bee returns home to the hive.

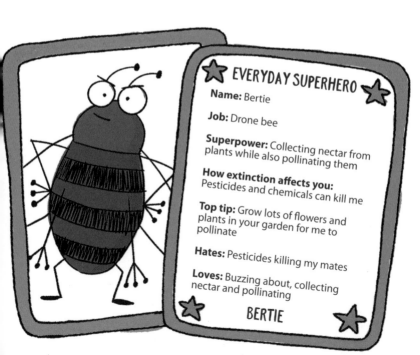

⭐ EVERYDAY SUPERHERO ⭐

Name: Bertie

Job: Drone bee

Superpower: Collecting nectar from plants while also pollinating them

How extinction affects you: Pesticides and chemicals can kill me

Top tip: Grow lots of flowers and plants in your garden for me to pollinate

Hates: Pesticides killing my mates

Loves: Buzzing about, collecting nectar and pollinating

BERTIE

OVERFISHING

Do you love eating fish? Me too. But unfortunately, it seems that bad fishing practices are having a terrible effect on some fish populations.

We have been eating fish for thousands of years. If we fish sensibly and don't take too much, it's fine. However, when we take too much, it's known as overfishing. That's when we get problems.

WHY IS IT CAUSING EXTINCTION?

Some fishing practices are OK because they leave plenty of fish in the sea. But when too many fish are taken it means that the number of fish decline. If young fish are taken it means there are no adults to reproduce. In some cases nets and lines catch other species – this is known as bycatch – and this can have a terrible effect on them too.

Time to call time on eating prawns!

BAD NEWS!!!
In fisheries where they use huge nets to catch prawns and fish they also catch other fish accidentally. What a waste!

POACHING AND TRAFFICKING FOR MEDICINE

Some people believe that parts of some animals can have health benefits if they use them as medicine.

The best-known example of this is the rhino. It is believed that consuming ground rhino horn can cure all kinds of diseases.

WHY IS IT CAUSING EXTINCTION?

When animals get used for medicine it means they have a value. The more people poach an animal, the more it is protected by law, the more it is worth and the more likely it is that the animals will face extinction.

BAD NEWS!!!
The pangolin is the most poached and trafficked animal on Earth. It is protected under international law but it is estimated that over a million of them were poached and sold in a ten-year period. Their scales are used in Chinese and Asian medicine, even though there is no evidence to suggest that they have any healing properties.

INVASIVE SPECIES

Ever since humans have been travelling around the world they have been bringing animals, plants and diseases with them, whether they meant to or not. Sometimes they bring animals to act as pests or to make life easier for themselves.

In the 1840s camels were imported to Australia as pack animals (to carry stuff). Once they were not needed any more they were set free. Now there are about a million of them living wild. The camels don't belong there and haven't evolved there, making life difficult for some of the native animals.

WHY IS IT CAUSING EXTINCTION?

While invasive species are often very successful, they put enormous pressure on native species, often sending them into decline. The grey squirrel is a fine example. It was imported into the UK in the 1870s from the USA. They brought with them a disease called the squirrel parapoxvirus, which is very dangerous to native red squirrels. As a result, and also because of the grey's success, the red squirrel has been displaced in most of the UK and is endangered.

GOOD NEWS!!!

The red squirrel's arch enemy, the pine marten is also endangered. But it has been discovered that pine martens find it easier to kill and eat grey squirrels than red squirrels. So where you find them, you are likely to find red squirrels too!

FARMING

Food production has had a huge effect on the planet. It's a struggle to feed everyone, which means we use more and more land to grow crops.

Farmers are also using more of the same crops around the world and using practices that exclude biodiversity because they turn over vast tracts of land to one crop.

WHY IS IT CAUSING EXTINCTION?

One of the problems with global food production is that it can put pressure on more traditional local varieties of fruit, vegetables and grains, which then die out. The more popular types of food take over, pushing out the local varieties.

On another level, farming single crops in large areas, with bigger fields and fewer hedges means that animals, birds, flowers and plants have nowhere to live. Crops don't provide food for many animals, which means animals that rely on them go hungry.

Soil health is important too. When land is ploughed it can lose its nutrients and the bacteria that live in the soil through erosion. This means the soil isn't healthy, which means more and more fertilizer is put on it. This endangers animals and plants that live nearby.

THE PLANET IN THE BALANCE

Now you've got to grips with extinction and what it means, your next mission is to learn to appreciate nature, how we are connected to it, and how it supports us every day. This mission is super easy and lots of fun and I hope you'll really enjoy it. And, in doing it, you might just help to save a few animals, birds and plants too.

ABOUT ECOSYSTEMS

The natural world is made up of thousands of ecosystems, communities of interconnected and interacting organisms, each of which supports life. Some ecosystems can be as big as the Amazon rainforest, with millions of plants, animals, fish and insects relying on each other for food, shelter and nutrients. Others can be as small as a garden pond. Ecosystems can be underwater, up a tree or under a log and can cover a huge area or can take up just a tiny space

QUICK QUIZ

Q: What's the world's biggest ecosystem?

ANSWERS: The World!

YOUR 2 MINUTE MISSION: Make a terrarium. It is a self-sustaining ecosystem. It's pretty easy to make one although you might need some help from an adult.
15 POINTS

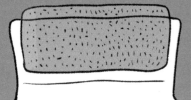

PLANT POWER: Plants make oxygen in the daytime by taking on carbon dioxide and water and using sunlight to turn it into carbon, which is new growth. At night they respire, like us, giving out water.

YOU WILL NEED:
A large glass jar that can be sealed; some gravel; some compost or mud; some water; some plants, like ferns.

1. Place the gravel in the bottom of the jar.
2. Place the earth on top.
3. Plant the fern.
4. Put some water in the bottom of the jar, then seal it.
5. Place the jar in a sunny spot and keep an eye on it. In time it should be self-sustaining because it has everything it needs: light, water, carbon dioxide.

FOOD CHAINS AND FOOD WEBS

Within every ecosystem there will be a food chain. It's called a chain because all the links in it are essential and, if one link were to break, the whole chain would fall apart.

If one part of the chain goes extinct – perhaps because humans have damaged their nest sites – then the balance is lost and everything falls apart.

When all the food chains in an ecosystem are joined up together, they form a food web. Food webs look more complex, but they are basically lots of chains connected together.

This is the way animals provide food for each other and how they benefit the ecosystem as a whole because everything in that ecosystem is important. It's easiest to explain when we talk about the sea.

LARGE SHARK

MACKEREL

PLANKTON

JUVENILE FISH

TINY ALGAE

TUNA

PRODUCERS AND CONSUMERS

A food chain always starts with a producer, an organism that makes food. This is usually a green plant, because plants can make their own food by photosynthesis using energy from the sun. A food chain ends with a consumer, an animal that eats a plant or another animal, such as a toothy shark.

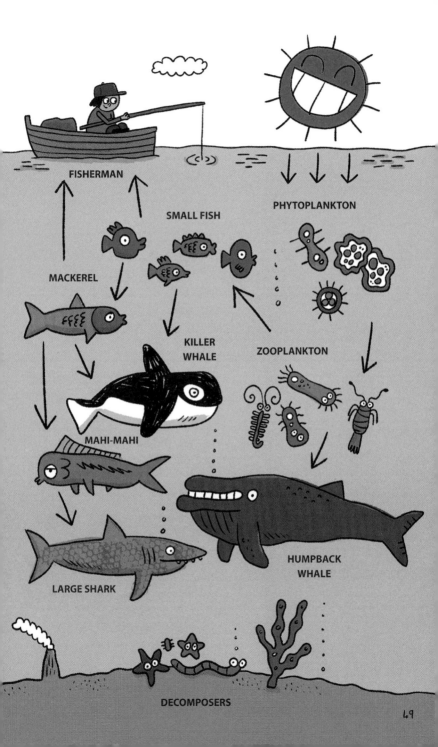

FISHERMAN

PHYTOPLANKTON

SMALL FISH

MACKEREL

KILLER
WHALE

ZOOPLANKTON

MAHI-MAHI

HUMPBACK
WHALE

LARGE SHARK

DECOMPOSERS

49

KEYSTONE SPECIES

Sharks are apex predators, which means they are at the top of the food chain. They are also keystone species, which means they are vitally important to keep the ecosystem in balance. Sharks help to keep the larger fish healthy and in balance (sharks are lazy and prefer to eat weak or injured fish) with the number of smaller fish below them in the food chain.

If you lose the sharks you lose the balance, which will change the ecosystem. It's also important to remember that each link in the food chain – I cannot emphasize this enough – is vitally important. Even the little guys – the plankton and the small fry – are essential for life on Earth. And if we lose any one of them, we lose everything.

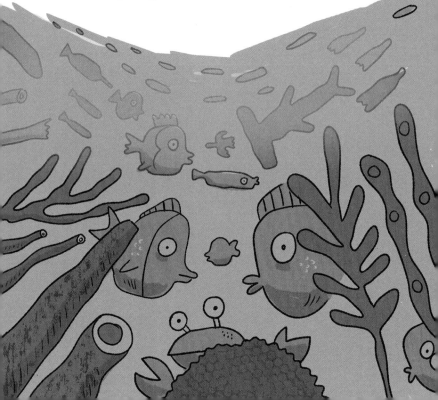

WHY YOU MATTER

You are important because you have some control over how
you live. Whenever you make decisions to look after nature or
to destroy it – to mow the lawn or let it grow longer – you have
an effect on nature.

Everything you do is important. It really is. And the sooner
you realize that, the sooner you'll be able to take your place on
the superhero podium as an extinction-fighting wonder kid
with a big heart and a love of nature who is super strong and
kind to animals. What more could you want to be?

51

FIGHT EXTINCTION FROM THE GROUND UP

Now that you've read the first few chapters of this book you should realize that extinction is a big problem all over the planet. You might also think that there's not much you can do for animals that are in danger in other parts of the world or that are struggling with problems that are too big for you to solve.

While you will probably grow up to be an awesome superhero and will be able to do this when you are older, you need to think about what you can do at home, right here, right now.

Let's start at ground level, with the little guys. I'm talking about the creepy-crawlies. They need your help!

WHAT ARE CREEPY-CRAWLIES?

Creepy-crawlies are all those little things that creep and crawl (obviously). They include insects, spiders, centipedes, snails, beetles, bees, wasps, worms, crabs and scorpions. They are usually known, collectively, as invertebrates, which means they don't have a spine (or backbone). And these are divided into those that have legs and those that don't. Some of them are beyond belief. Some are so small you can hardly see them. Some are beautiful. All of them are amazing.

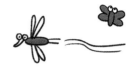

BE A FRIEND TO CREEPY-CRAWLIES

Even if creepy-crawlies scare you I'd like you to at least begin to try to understand how wonderful, different, mad and amazing they are. Make friends with them. Let them have their space and don't get too close if you don't want to. Just don't stamp on them!!! We need them as much as they need us to look after them. It's that simple. Let's start work!!!

YOUR 2 MINUTE MISSION: Go outside and see if you can find any creepy-crawlies. Don't get too close or touch them, especially if you are afraid of them. Replace any stones carefully and try not to harm any of them. **10 POINTS**

FEARFUL FACT: Are you terrified of ten footed centipedes? Freaked out by flies? Spooked by spiders? It could be that you are entomophobic. This is having a fear of insects.

YOU WILL NEED:
- An open mind
- Some outdoor space
- A magnifying glass
- A notepad
- A smartphone
- Maybe also some kneepads

53

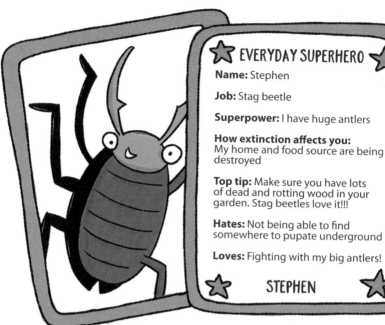

Name: Stephen

Job: Stag beetle

Superpower: I have huge antlers

How extinction affects you:
My home and food source are being destroyed

Top tip: Make sure you have lots of dead and rotting wood in your garden. Stag beetles love it!!!

Hates: Not being able to find somewhere to pupate underground

Loves: Fighting with my big antlers!

STEPHEN

FACT: Stag beetle numbers are becoming rarer in the UK and their numbers are declining in Europe. They are already extinct in some places.

YOUR 2 MINUTE MISSION: **Get to know your creepy-crawlies better. Books can help you identify insects. Apps are great at helping you find out what they do and how they act. (Beware: some may have in-app purchases). 5 POINTS**

CREEPY-CRAWLY FACT: Scientists have found around a million insect species. Incredibly, scientists estimate that there are about 4 million species yet to be named!

WHY ARE CREEPY-CRAWLIES IMPORTANT?

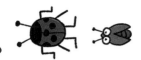

Invertebrates are vital to life on Earth. They live everywhere. In your house, in the garden, in the fields and in the oceans. They provide food for larger animals and birds, act as pollinators (which means they fertilize plants) and also act as nature's great recyclers, turning dead plants and animals into healthy, life giving soil. If the invertebrates go we won't be able to grow crops, won't have healthy soil and will also lose lots more of the birds and animals that rely on them for food.

THE UNKNOWN APOCALYPSE

It's easy to understand the extinction of big animals like elephants, but it's a lot harder to get to grips with insects. Partly because we don't know so much about them but also because it's hard to count them. We don't know how many have gone, although it is estimated that we have lost about 60% of the world's population of invertebrates since 1976.

WHY ARE CREEPY-CRAWLIES FACING EXTINCTION?

HABITAT LOSS: Invertebrates are also under threat because of habitat loss where hedgerows are destroyed, forests felled and agricultural land is expanded.

POLLUTION: Pollution, from factories, industry and transport is also another risk to invertebrates.

CLIMATE CHANGE: Adverse weather, warming seas and changing seasonal averages can cause terrible problems for some insect populations.

PESTICIDES: Lots of insects and invertebrates are viewed as parasites and pests by the farming industry because they can destroy food crops. As a result, we have invented pesticides and chemicals that kill creepy-crawlies in their millions.

YOUR 2 MINUTE MISSION: Weedkiller is terrible for insects and invertebrates. Ask your parents, school and local council to stop using it, if they do. You can write letters and emails or even start a protest. 10 POINTS

CREEPY-CRAWLY FACT: People who study insects are called entomologists. What does that make you, as someone who saves them? A superheroentomologist, of course!

You superhero bug lover you!

YOUR 2 MINUTE MISSION: Name your pet spider. Spiders are great. So, next time you find one, don't harm it. Give it a name, let it do its stuff and be its friend. 10 POINTS

YOUR 2 MINUTE MISSION: Inspire your friends to take care of insects too. Could you dress up like an insect? Or maybe you could write a story about your pet spider? 10 POINTS

WEBBY TIP: House spiders, funnily enough, only live inside houses, which means they don't survive outside. They are largely harmless to us and help by eating flies and insects that come inside.

57

FIGHT EXTINCTION IN YOUR GARDEN

Do you have a garden? If you do, then great, this chapter is for you. But even if you only have a little outside space – a balcony or yard – then it's still possible to fight extinction with it too. That's because everything you do makes a difference. I know I keep telling you this but it's important for you to remember that you are important, that you matter and that the things you do have an effect on the planet and all the animals in it. Even if it's just something tiny, it still counts.

NATURE WILL FIND A WAY

Nature is incredible. Somehow it will find a way to inhabit your spaces, whether you like it or not! Notice how plants grow in between the cracks in the pavements or how adults get annoyed by "weeds" growing everywhere. Once nature gets hold it's difficult to keep it down – and that's fantastic.

YOUR 2 MINUTE MISSION: Can you see plants growing in the cracks in the pavement, in gaps in walls and in spaces that are unloved or forgotten? Isn't it amazing how nature always seems to find a way to grow – no matter how hard we make it! 5 POINTS

BEWARE THE INVADERS!!!

Sometimes, nature has a habit of going a bit mad and taking over, especially when it comes to plants and animals that aren't supposed to be there. Invasive species – which are from other countries or continents brought here accidentally or on purpose – are like the naughty kids from another school. They don't understand the rules and just do what they want, when they want. What it means is that native plants find it hard to find their space – in fact it's been completely taken over! This can lead to local plants and wildlife struggling to survive.

GET TO KNOW THE BAD GUYS!

Japanese knotweed:
Pointed leaves. Red stems in spring. Looks a bit like bamboo. Grows up to 2cm a day.

Himalayan balsam:
Long, pointed leaves with serrated edges. Flowers can be white, pink and purple with five petals. Produces lots of nectar so bees love it and ignore other plants.

Three-cornered leek:
Comes up in spring. Looks a bit like a white bluebell. Stems are triangular. Smells of garlic!

YOUR 2 MINUTE MISSION: Take this book outside and see if you can spot any invasive species. If it's Japanese knotweed you'll need to tell an adult. It is a controlled substance and allowing it to spread can result in big fines! 10 POINTS

FLOWERS WITHOUT LOVE. WHY WEEDS ARE ADORABLE!!!

Did you know that weeds are just plants that haven't found love yet? It's true. Lots of people consider some plants as weeds and get rid of them from their gardens. It's terribly sad! Lots of these misunderstood plants are AMAZING for wildlife because of the food they provide for the birds and insects and the pollen they produce for bees.

Some weeds are invasive and spread quickly, which means they aren't good for birds and insects, but others can be fantastic and help your garden or outdoor space.

YOUR 2 MINUTE MISSION: Download a plant identification app. Then go out into the garden or park and try to identify a few plants. Are they considered weeds? Are they friend or foe? You decide, based on how you think they help the natural world. **10 POINTS**

SOME FRIENDS SOME CALL FOES:

Daisy:
Lovely white flowers that many consider a weed. But insects and bees – and birds – love them!

White clover:
This little plant is great for everyone as it is good for the soil and creepy-crawlies. And that's food for the birds.

Dandelion:
When bumblebees come out of hibernation in spring, dandelions are often the first thing they seek because they are the first flowers.

BE KIND TO BEES

They might be small, but bees are mighty. They are pollinators, which means that they are vital when it comes to helping plants produce fruit. Sounds complicated? Sorry. Let me explain. Bees love the nectar and pollen produced by flowers. They visit lots of them, collecting it, either for themselves or for their hives.

When they do this, they carry pollen on the hairs of their bodies to other plants of the same species. These bits of pollen then rub off on the reproductive parts of the new plants and fertilize them. Once this has happened the plant can grow fruit and the plant's lifecycle can continue.

UN-BEE-LIEVABLE FACTS:

♠ There are thousands of bee species around the world. Many of them are specialists and have adapted to pollinate certain plants. If those bees die the plants would die too.

♠ Bees are vital to us because it is estimated they pollinate up to a third of the crops we need for food. Without them we'd go hungry.

♠ Humans also cultivate bees for their honey and the wax they make in their hives. Without them, no honey!

YOUR 2 MINUTE MISSION: In the autumn, plant a bee-friendly flower pot with bulbs of crocus, snowdrop, grape hyacinth and scented daffodil. The bulbs will produce flowers in spring when the bees need them most. 30 POINTS

WHY BEES ARE THREATENED WITH EXTINCTION

All kinds of bees – from honey bees to solitary bees and bumblebees – are under threat. According to Friends of the Earth, the UK has lost thirteen species of bee, with more under threat. The reasons are numerous but include the loss of habitats that bees love (since the 1930s the UK has lost over 95% of wildflower meadows), the use of pest-killing insecticides and herbicides (harmful chemicals that kill insect pests also kill bees), climate change (bees can be confused by seasons changing early or late and their favourite flowers being in bloom at the wrong time) and invasive species and disease (the Asian hornet, for example, is deadly to British bees).

YOUR 2 MINUTE MISSION: Make a bee hotel. 50 POINTS

YOU WILL NEED:

An old fizzy pop bottle or a plastic tube, about 10cm long; lengths of bamboo in different diameters, about 8cm long; some wire; some plasticine.

1. Choose pieces of bamboo with single or no knots in. If there are no knots, block up one end with plasticine.
2. Fill the bottle with the lengths of bamboo, adding enough so they don't fall out and so that the tube overhangs the ends.
3. Place in the garden somewhere sunny, facing south and about a metre off the ground. Leave alone. In spring the bees will find your hotel and lay their eggs. The following year the new bees will emerge!!

⭐ EVERYDAY SUPERHERO ⭐

Name: Buzz (what else?)

Job: Bumblebee

Superpower: I buzz about carrying pollen between plants to fertilize them

How extinction affects you:
The places I live are under threat. Weedkiller kills my pals too

Top tip: Stop using weedkiller and plant more flowers

Hates: That wildflower meadows are getting rarer

Loves: Buzzing around lots of flowers

⭐ BUZZ ⭐

YOUR 2 MINUTE MISSION: Let dandelions grow in your garden. Dandelions are among the first flowers to bloom in spring. That means bees can get a jolly good feast on nectar soon after a long winter or hibernation. 10 POINTS

LOVE YOUR LAWN

Did you know that your lawn may well be the second greatest weapon you have in your battle to fight extinction. Yes! Lawns are places that can either be without much life and biodiversity or that can be full of wildlife, flowers and, under the surface, worms, grubs and insects. Grass that is cut longer and left to grow for longer between cuts is better for the planet and is a great way to help fight extinction from your own garden!

WHAT'S THE PROBLEM WITH LAWNS?

When lawns are cut short, free of weeds and treated with pesticides and lawn treatments they are like green deserts because they don't provide much of a home for wildlife, insects or grubs and snails. They might look smart and neat but they can't support a huge amount of biodiversity – something we now know is vital for nature to thrive.

YOUR 2 MINUTE MISSION: **Talk to the mower in your family about mowing every three weeks, instead of every week. 10 POINTS**

SAY NO MOW TO SHORTER LAWNS!

YOUR LOCAL LAWNS

Even if you don't have a lawn at home you can make a difference to the lawns in your street or town. You can do this by writing to your local council to ask them to consider leaving verges and parks longer than usual or to change their mowing regime to allow for flowers to grow.

You could also ask people in your street to let the grass grow longer too. Some of them might change their habits when you point out the advantages of leaving their lawns to grow a little longer.

YOUR 2 MINUTE MISSION: Make a flyer to put in the letterboxes in your street asking people to cut down their mowing from once a week to once every three weeks. Make it colourful and don't forget to include facts from this book. 10 POINTS

FACT: Researchers found that mowing lawns less often increases biodiversity, saves money and reduces weeds!

FIGHT EXTINCTION AT THE BIRD TABLE

Recently, scientists reported that 40% of the world's 11,000 bird species are in decline, and one in eight bird species is threatened with global extinction. In the UK it is estimated that 35% of birds are under threat or are declining. Even the house sparrow has seen a decline over decades. Imagine not seeing them in your gardens! It's unthinkable. Isn't it?

There are lots of reasons why birds are endangered. Listing them reads like a history of mankind, unfortunately, as more often than not they are caused by us. Of course, the good news is that it means we can stop the decline if we act together and quickly.

⭐ EVERYDAY SUPERHERO ⭐

Name: Kaia

Job: North Island brown kiwi

Superpower: I am so rare that there were only a handful of my kind left around 30 years ago

How extinction affects you: My eggs were getting eaten by invasive species like stoats

Top tip: Support kiwi rescue charities

Hates: Dogs that chase me

Loves: The New Zealand rainforest

 KAIA

WHAT CAUSES BIRDS TO GO EXTINCT?

INVASIVE SPECIES:
Some birds are extremely vulnerable to invasive species. Birds, like the gorgeous but very flightless kākāpō, are especially vulnerable, because invasive species like stoats and rats make easy prey of them.

LOSS OF HABITAT:
All over the world bird habitats are being lost to human development or agriculture, leaving many birds with nowhere to live. The tree sparrow has declined by 95% due to the loss of hedgerows and more aggressive farming practices in the UK.

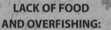

LACK OF FOOD AND OVERFISHING:
Atlantic puffins are endangered because warming seas and overfishing have reduced the number of fish in their habitat, leaving them hungry and at risk.

CHEMICALS AND POLLUTANTS:
When birds eat food that is contaminated with chemicals, those chemicals can build up in their bodies and eventually kill them. The California condor is at risk because of lead pollution from shot game it was eating.

HOW TO HELP THE BIRDS IN YOUR GARDEN

Lots of birds live among us in towns, cities and in the countryside. In difficult times – the winter or early spring – they can sometimes struggle to find food. For many birds the threats they face are due to lack of food because of declining habitats.

You might think that birds should be able to survive losing their habitats, wouldn't you? After all, birds can (mostly) fly. The problem, however, is when the habitat provides food that can't be found anywhere else. If a bird is specialized or has a special kind of food – that exists only in one habitat – then the loss of that habitat will inevitably mean food is more scarce and survival harder for the birds.

YOUR 2 MINUTE MISSION: Make a birdy cake for the birds to eat! It's really easy (but you might need to get a little help from one of your pet adults). 30 POINTS

YOU WILL NEED:
100g lard; 200g bird seeds; clean plastic yoghurt pots.

1. In a pan, melt 100g of lard.
2. Add in 200g of bird seeds and nuts, dried fruit, oatmeal and bits of cake.
3. When it has cooled a bit, but before it sets, pour out into a few clean plastic yoghurt pots.
4. When the cakes have set, prize them out of the pots and put them (one at a time) on your bird table.

YOUR 2 MINUTE MISSION Make a bird cafe. It can be as simple as hanging birdy cakes off a hook on your balcony. But if you have help and a few bits of wood, it's easy. **50 POINTS**

YOU WILL NEED:
1m long piece of wood; a board 30cm square;
four small pieces of wood 1cm high; screws; hooks; a drill.

1. Find a length of wood for the base with one end that is flat. This needs to be at least 1m tall. Dig a hole and plant it so it's upright and there is at least 1m of it out of the ground.
2. Find a piece of board that is about 30cm square. Attach a wooden rim around the edges of the board at least 1cm high, leaving gaps at the corners.
3. Fix the board to the upright piece of wood.
4. Screw hooks into the board so you can hang fat cakes or feeders from them. Ta da! A bird cafe!!!

YOUR 2 MINUTE MISSION: Take a book out of the library or download an app and learn to identify the birds that visit your bird cafe. **10 POINTS**

FIGHT EXTINCTION WITH WATER

We take water for granted, don't we? I know I do. It comes out of my tap and falls from the sky above my house. When I hear about animals losing their fight with extinction it leaks from my eyes too.

It's simple. Water is life and without it we would all perish. We need it to drink, to wash, to cook. Nature needs water too. Plants need it to grow, animals need it to drink and wash. Insects need it for their life cycle. Amphibians need it to lay their eggs. Fish need it to swim in!!!

It seems, sometimes, like there is water everywhere. And if there is, why do we need to use it to help us fight extinction?

WHY SAVING WATER IS IMPORTANT

There are lots of reasons why it's important we don't waste water. Firstly, water from the tap costs money, so the less you use the less your parents have to pay.

Secondly, water takes energy and effort to filter, clean and pump to your house, so it saves carbon (and helps fight climate change) when you use less. The less water you use at home the less water has to be taken out of nature (rivers, reservoirs and lakes) and the more there is for animals and plants.

Thirdly, nature doesn't always like the clean, pure water and prefers rain water. That's because water from our taps is too clean for some plants and creatures.

SAVING RAINWATER

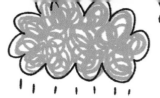

Are you growing plants or vegetables? If you are, then you will have to give them water at some point or they will die. Instead of giving them water from the tap, it's much better to give them rainwater you have collected. It's cheaper too.

YOUR 2 MINUTE MISSION: **Harvesting rainwater is really easy to do. Put out a bucket on your windowsill, balcony or in the garden and see how much water you collect when it rains. Save it and use it to water your plants, either indoors or outdoors, when they need it. 10 POINTS**

HARVESTING MORE THAN JUST A BUCKET

The bigger the area you can collect water from the more water you'll be able to harvest. Roofs are excellent places to collect rainwater from as they collect a lot of water. Putting a bucket or a big container like a water barrel underneath a drainpipe can collect lots of water very quickly. It's not that easy to set up so you will have to talk to your parents or carers. Try to explain that it will help to save money.

YOUR 2 MINUTE MISSION: **Speak to your parents or carers about setting up a water barrel. If you grow plants it will be useful to water them with. 10 POINTS**

WHY PONDS ARE AMAZING

Ponds are incredible mini ecosystems that can support all kinds of plants, insects, animals and birds. They can be big or they can be tiny. Even the smallest ponds can attract insects and amphibians and become little worlds in themselves that are self-sufficient and don't need much looking after. They become homes for insects that need water for their life cycle and provide a nursery for animals that need it to breed. Ponds can also help to support lots of life around them by providing food.

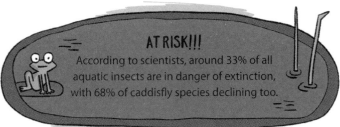

AT RISK!!!

According to scientists, around 33% of all aquatic insects are in danger of extinction, with 68% of caddisfly species declining too.

⭐ EVERYDAY SUPERHERO ⭐

Name: Claire

Job: Caddisfly

Superpower: I live as a larvae and cover myself in a protective suit of stones and pebbles

How extinction affects you: We are losing our homes too and without water we won't survive

Top tip: Make us a pond!!!

Hates: That ponds are disappearing

Loves: Living in your little pond, safe from harm, getting ready to fly away!

⭐ CLAIRE ⭐

MAKE YOUR OWN POND!

Making a pond can be really simple. The simplest ponds are just containers with rainwater (that you have saved). Even if you don't have a garden, you could still talk to your teacher about making a pond at school. Explain to your classmates why it's important and get them to help. It would be a great project!!

YOUR 2 MINUTE MISSION: Make a simple washing up bowl pond. 10 POINTS

YOU WILL NEED:
An old, watertight washing up bowl; two different native plants in pots; some gravel and stones; a spade.

1. Firstly, dig a hole in your garden where people won't fall into it and where it won't always be in the sun. A partly shady corner is perfect. Make it big enough so that the bowl will fit into it and the top of the bowl will be level with the ground.
2. Place some clean gravel in the bottom of the bowl. Add some stones into the bowl to be like steps so that frogs and newts can get in and out.
3. Fill it up with rainwater. Keep it topped up.

WHAT WILL YOU FIND IN YOUR POND?

Wait and see what arrives in your pond. Your pond might take a little time to get established. But that's OK. It may take a few weeks for insects and amphibians to find it. Keep looking though, and see what you find.

FIGHT EXTINCTION IN THE SUPERMARKET

You might not expect to see many animals in the supermarket. In fact, you may not see any animals at all when you go shopping. Can you imagine an orangutan swinging from the ceiling in the toiletry aisle? I thought not.

But, believe it or not, you can help orangutans – and a whole lot of other plants and animals – by helping with the shopping. When you help out at the supermarket, or better still, at your local shops, you'll be able to influence the choices your family makes and that could, in turn, help nature.

In some ways, the way your family shops might well be one of the most powerful weapons you have in your fight against extinction.

Let me explain.

HOW CAN YOUR SHOPPING AFFECT EXTINCTION?

All our food has to be grown or caught. From corn flakes to rump steak, everything has a story: where and how it's grown, how it's caught, reared or trapped, how it's treated while it's growing and where it has come from to get to you. It's that story that is vitally important when it comes to extinction.

THE STORY OF YOUR FOOD

Do you know where your food comes from?
Which of the following do you think is best for nature?

COW 1: Reared on land created by cutting down rainforests.

COW 2: Reared on an intensive farm in the UK. Fed on GM soy from Brazil.

Meat is shipped to the supermarket by boat or plane.

Meat travels to the supermarket in big lorries.

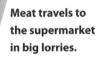

Meat is sold at your local farmers' market.

COW 3: Reared on a farm in UK. Fed on a wildflower meadow, outside.

HOW MUCH!!??

When it comes to budgeting, eating "sustainable" food presents difficult choices as it is often more expensive. So don't put pressure on your parents or carers to buy organic food if the budget doesn't allow. That's not fair on them. However, what you can do is learn to cook from fresh ingredients and fruit and veg which can be really cheap and will help you in your mission to fight extinction. Find out more in mission 9.

FISH
EGGS
APPLES
BREAD

YOUR 2 MINUTE MISSION: Find a food that your family eats regularly. Check out the ingredients. If it's GM or has palm oil in it, find an alternative, if you can. Do a price comparison. Is it cheaper or more expensive? 10 POINTS

WHEN FOOD CAUSES EXTINCTIONS

In some parts of the world forest is cleared to make way for agriculture and for rearing livestock. This is having a devastating effect on nature because it deprives all the native species of a home, forcing them into smaller and smaller pockets of forest.

SAYONARA TO THE JUNGLE: Since 2016, an average of 28 million hectares or rainforest have been cut down every year. That's one football field of forest lost every single second around the clock.

Even in the UK and Europe our food production is causing extinctions. Pesticides are polluting our rivers and soils and hedgerows are being torn up to make bigger and bigger fields of single crops. This results in a loss of biodiversity as animals and plants have nowhere to live and no food.

ADIEU TO THE MEADOWS: Since the 1930s the UK has lost around 97% of its wildflower meadows due to increases in food production. Wildflower meadows are vital to pollinators and the animals that feed on them.

When it comes to food caught in the sea, it's a similar problem. Nets used to target one species of fish often catch lots of other fish along the way, including dolphins, whales and other animals at risk of extinction. This is known as bycatch.

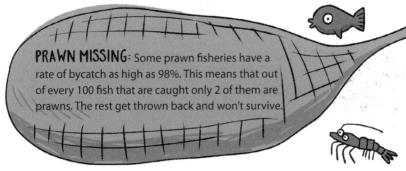

PRAWN MISSING: Some prawn fisheries have a rate of bycatch as high as 98%. This means that out of every 100 fish that are caught only 2 of them are prawns. The rest get thrown back and won't survive.

Also, lots of smaller species of fish are targeted to make food for farmed salmon. Farmed salmon takes about 1.5kg of fish to grow 1kg of meat. That's a bit mad isn't it? Farming salmon has a bad effect on local wildlife because of disease and pollution. Overfishing also steals food from seabirds and fish, helping to drive them closer to extinction.

WHEN SCIENCE ALSO CAUSES EXTINCTIONS

Humans have been working for years to "design" crops that are resistant to drought and disease. This is known as genetic modification (GM). It makes sense if we can grow more to feed all 7 billion of us, right? Well, yes. It does.

But some companies modify crops for profit and to control the market. They sell seeds that have been modified to be pesticide resistant or will produce crops under difficult conditions.

This means that farmers can use pesticides on crops and it won't kill them. The pesticides will only kill pests and, sadly, pollinators, bees and insects. These pesticides can accumulate in the ground and ruin the health of the soil, killing worms and invertebrates in the process.

Another problem with GM crops is that they are infertile, which means the farmer has to buy the seeds every year instead of saving a few of his grains for the following year. This means that local varieties of the crops die out because all the crops are the same.

YOUR 2 MINUTE MISSION: Add organic material such as compost to your garden. Worms are the heroes of the mud. They recycle dead matter – like leaves and dead flowers – and turn it into healthy, nutrient-rich soil that's great for growing. **20 POINTS**

WHAT DOES ALL THIS MEAN?

Our shopping is vital in the fight against extinction. If we make good choices then we can support positive and sustainable food production. If we make bad choices – buying GM foods or products that are grown on rainforest land or reared unsustainably – we aren't helping at all. Who'd have thought your shopping could be so important!

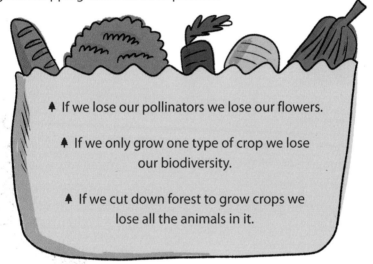

♠ If we lose our pollinators we lose our flowers.

♠ If we only grow one type of crop we lose our biodiversity.

♠ If we cut down forest to grow crops we lose all the animals in it.

WHAT CAN YOU DO ABOUT IT?

It's all about choices. The choices you make now may help to define the future of lots of plants, animals, insects and ecosystems. Buying fresh, seasonal and local ingredients is the very best way to fight extinction. Buying from local shops, butchers, fishmongers and markets is by far the best way to do this. It can be more fun too. You get to meet nice people, talk about where food comes from and maybe even learn some lovely new recipes.

LOOK AT THE LABELS

The labels on food can tell you a lot of stuff, from the calories to sugar and fat content. By law labels have to say whether or not a food stuff contains ingredients that are genetically modified. And they should tell you the country of origin too.

> YOUR 2 MINUTE MISSION: **While you might not be able to change what your family buys, you can look at the labels on the food they buy. Check it out. See where it comes from. Take a look at some of the ingredients they use. 10 POINTS**

SOYA SO WHAT!

Soya is an ingredient that's in lots of food and that is used to feed livestock. It takes a lot of soy beans to grow a steak. Most of it is grown in the USA or Brazil. Some is grown in Europe. In Brazil the rainforest and savannahs – important ecosystems for biodiversity – are being turned into soy plantations. This means the local biodiversity is lost, animals lose their homes, many lose their food and lots lose their lives, getting ever closer to extinction.

> YOUR 2 MINUTE MISSION: **Check out the labels of foods you suspect may have soya. It may be difficult. But if it says it's from Brazil, avoid it. 10 POINTS**

PALM US OFF ON PALM OIL

Palm oil is another ingredient that is in a lot of foods, such as cereals, hot chocolate, crisps, noodles and pizza. It's everywhere! The trouble is that there is such demand for it that rainforest is being cut down to grow it. This leaves lots of animals without homes or food. Orangutans are endangered particularly because of deforestation due to the spread of agriculture.

YOUR 2 MINUTE MISSION: Look at the labels on your shopping. See if you can spot the palm oil. 10 POINTS

⭐ **EVERYDAY SUPERHERO** ⭐

Name: Mubaraka

Job: Orangutan

Superpower: I have really long arms! The bigger males have arm spans that are over 2 metres. That's about 7 feet!

How extinction affects you: My home is being chopped down to grow palm oil

Top tip: You can help me by not eating food with palm oil in

Hates: Seeing bulldozers in my forest

Loves: Living a quiet life in the trees with my kids and family

⭐ **MUBARAKA** ⭐

MISSION 9
FIGHT EXTINCTION IN THE KITCHEN

How's your cooking? Is it any good? Can you whip up a wicked lunch? I bet you can!! If you can't, don't worry, you can learn. It's fun to cook and it's great for you, the planet and nature if you cook with fresh, local and seasonal ingredients. And it'll be tastier too!

We already talked about going to the shops and buying your food. Hopefully you've got a whole pile of super fresh, local and seasonal vegetables from your trip to the shops. Now what are you going to do with it?

FUN FOODIE FACTS:

Kale is full of vitamin A and C, iron and calcium, which means it is great for your hair!!! So eat them up!!!

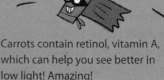

Carrots contain retinol, vitamin A, which can help you see better in low light! Amazing!

Broccoli contains more protein than steak. What???! Yes! Munch on those tiny green trees!!!

Apples contain fructose, which is a natural sugar. So it could be better at waking you up than coffee!

ALL SUPERHEROES NEED SUPER FOODS!

We've already talked about why it's important to look at the ingredients in your food. So let's now look at the effect your diet can have on nature.

EATING LOCALLY

The more you eat locally the more you will be able to fight extinction. Local varieties of plants and animals are bred and adapted to growing well where you are. Also, they provide food for, and support, insects and birds that are also adapted for life near you.

YOUR 2 MINUTE MISSION: Apples are grown all over the world. But here in the UK there are a few varieties that are native. See if you can find them in your local shops. 10 POINTS

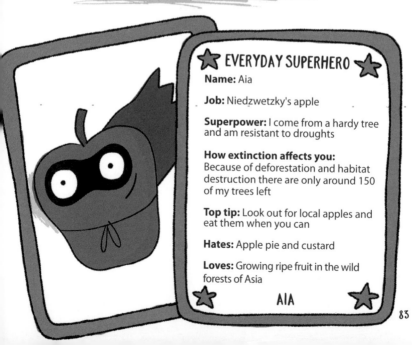

⭐ **EVERYDAY SUPERHERO** ⭐

Name: Aia

Job: Niedzwetzky's apple

Superpower: I come from a hardy tree and am resistant to droughts

How extinction affects you:
Because of deforestation and habitat destruction there are only around 150 of my trees left

Top tip: Look out for local apples and eat them when you can

Hates: Apple pie and custard

Loves: Growing ripe fruit in the wild forests of Asia

AIA

EATING FISH

Fish is a superfood, fit for all kinds of superheroes, but it can be problematic. We know that some types of fish, like prawns and farmed salmon, are bad for the planet and can be contributors to the decline in biodiversity. But what about other types of fish?

The Marine Conservation Society compiles a list called the Good Fish Guide which tells you if a kind of fish is OK to eat because there are lots of them. It's useful. However, the only true way to buy fish is to only buy sustainably caught fish from the sea near where you live.

YOUR 2 MINUTE MISSION: **Look at your favourite fish dish and then go and look at www.mcsuk.org/goodfishguide to see how your fish fared on the Good Fish Guide. Did it do OK? Great!!! Not so good?? Maybe it's time to change brand or try something different. 20 POINTS**

EATING MEAT

Some people don't eat meat because they believe that meat production is bad in all kinds of ways. But it's not always as simple as you might think. Yes, meat reared on big farms and fed with soya grown on rainforest plantations in Brazil isn't such a good choice. But buying meat that's been reared on natural grassland can be OK, if you are OK with eating animals.

The solution? Eating meat all the time is expensive and not so great for your health, so it's a good idea to limit your meat eating. Eat home grown, free range, sustainably reared meat if you can.

WHY VEGANISM CAN BE GOOD FOR THE PLANET

Being vegan means not eating any kind of animal product. That includes eggs, milk, meat and fish. It can be a really healthy way to eat as it means eating lots of vegetables. But it can bring its own problems because it often means eating food imported from the other side of the world – and that's bad for the climate. Veganism is VERY good if you eat local.

YOUR 2 MINUTE MISSION: **Go vegan for a day. I bet you'll find that you'll get to love being a plant-based superhero. If you like it, why not go vegan one day each week? 50 POINTS**

EATING DAIRY

Drinking milk and eating cheese, yoghurt and butter has a lot of health benefits. But it also comes with the problems of lost habitats, pollution and losing biodiversity. Tough choices!!!

YOUR 2 MINUTE MISSION: **Make oat milk and try it on your cereal. It's the very best milk for the planet. 40 POINTS**

YOU WILL NEED:
128g of oats; 750ml water; a pinch of salt; a blender; muslin or a clean T-shirt.

1. Take 128g of oats and soak in fresh tap water for four hours. Strain the oats, rinse, discard the water and place the oats into a blender.
2. Add 750ml of fresh water and a tiny pinch of salt. WHIZZ IT UP! Until it's all smooth for 2–4 minutes.
3. Strain the milk through a muslin or clean T shirt. Drink! Do you like it?

85

FIGHT EXTINCTION IN THE BATHROOM

I know what you are thinking: what on Earth has my bathroom got to do with extinction?

Sadly, it has.

That's because of the products that you might find in it.

From soaps, skin care and shampoo to make up, deodorants and sunscreen, many of the products on the market contain palm oil.

Palm oil is good for moisturising, cleansing and conditioning, which is why so many companies use it. It's also cheap, which means it's good for their profits. Not so good for the planet though.

Happily some companies do make sustainable palm oil. They are usually marked with the Roundtable on Sustainable Palm Oil (RSPO) logo. It looks like this:

FACT: In the last 20 years almost 80% of the habitat of the orangutan has been lost to palm oil plantations. And it's not just the orangutans. Millions of indigenous people, who depend on the rainforest, have lost their forest homes too.

CHEMICALS IN YOUR BATHROOM

Good bathroom products rely on chemicals to clean our skin, teeth and hair. The problem occurs when those products get flushed down the loo or drain. They go down the sewage system and, eventually, into rivers and the sea.

Every drain in every house has a direct connection to the sea, even if they are hundreds of miles away. The trouble is that those chemicals go there too, and can cause harm to animals and fish on the way. River systems – and all that live in them – can be effectively killed because of pollution, although your shampoo is unlikely to have such a drastic effect. However, it all adds up and the less we use of harmful chemicals the better.

THINK BEFORE YOU FLUSH!

PLASTIC DANGER

Plastic that gets into the ocean, like cotton bud sticks or sanitary ware, can be a danger to wildlife, particularly turtles, which are endangered. Turtles mistake plastic bags for their favourite food, jelly fish, while seabirds mistake plastic fragments for fish. Plastic micro beads – tiny pieces of plastics in some beauty products – can also end up in the ocean where they become toxic and harm fish and animals that eat them.

YOUR 2 MINUTE MISSION: **Visit a waste-free shop. They have lots of products that are plastic-free and good for the planet. Look for soap that's doesn't contain palm oil and shampoo bars that you can rub on your head! 20 POINTS**

⭐ EVERYDAY SUPERHERO ⭐

Name: Larry

Job: Leatherback turtle

Superpower: I am huge!!! The biggest ever recorded was 10ft long!!!

How extinction affects you: I am in danger because of plastic bags and plastic pollution

Top tip: Think about what products you use in the bathroom

Hates: Plastic bags that look like jellyfish

Loves: Swimming in the open ocean

⭐ **LARRY** ⭐

YOUR 2 MINUTE MISSION: Done your missions? Good. Now it's time to have some superhero fun. Relax with an eco-friendly, home-made, luxury bath bomb. 50 POINTS

Warning: Be careful when it comes to mixing up the wet and dry ingredients – as a bath bomb can go off at any moment!!! Get some help getting the ingredients together and take your time.

YOU WILL NEED:

100g bicarbonate of soda; 50g citric acid; 25g cornflour; 25g Epsom salt (optional); 2 tbsp olive oil; ¼ tsp essential oil, such as lavender; a few drops of liquid food colouring; a mixing bowl; a whisk; clean moulds to shape your bath bomb.

1. Wash and dry your hands. Put the bicarbonate of soda, citric acid, cornflour and Epsom salt in a large mixing bowl, and mix it well.
2. Pour the olive oil, essential oil and food colouring into another, smaller bowl. Mix together.
3. Very slowly add the oil mixture into the dry mixture a little at a time and whisking between each addition. When it's all mixed together add a few drops of water – about half a tea spoon in total – and whizz it quickly to stop it from fizzing too much. CAREFUL. This is the important bit. You need the mixture to clump together but not be too wet.
4. Press the mixture into your moulds with your hands and then put in the fridge to dry and harden for four to five hours (or overnight). Remove it from the mould, run the bath and pull the pin!!!
5. Dive in and watch it fizz.

FIGHT EXTINCTION WITH YOUR POCKET MONEY

Sometimes, when the animals facing extinction are far away, struggling for survival in countries you may never see for yourself, it's difficult to fight for them directly. However, you can help the people who help them by supporting the work they do.

Giving money to charities that are involved in conservation work is a good way of helping animals that can't help themselves.

If you get pocket money you could donate a part of it to conservation charities or save up to adopt an animal.

You could even start a fundraiser at school to help fund research and conservation efforts!

Imagine that! Your school could help save the life of a gorilla, orangutan or even a blue whale!!!!

What an amazing thing you could do!

YOUR 2 MINUTE MISSION: Find an empty glass jar and a sticker. Write FOR FIGHTING EXTINCTION on the sticker and then stick it on the jar. Every time you have change, put it in the jar. When the jar is full, empty it and donate it to charity. 30 POINTS

ADOPT AN ANIMAL

You can "adopt" an animal, either in the wild or in your local zoo or conservation area. This means paying a monthly fee to help pay for protection and wardens to look after them (in the wild) or for food and lodgings (if they are in a zoo). If you adopt an endangered animal in a zoo then you might even be able to visit them!

> **YOUR 2 MINUTE MISSION:** You could use your pocket money to adopt an animal. Work out how much you can save each week and then put it in your EXTINCTION BANK to use later to adopt your favourite animal. **20 POINTS**

CAN'T DONATE MONEY? DONATE THINGS INSTEAD!

If you don't get pocket money or don't have money you can spare (it's OK – lots of people don't either) then you could always donate your things or time. Clothes you have grown out of or toys you don't need any more can be sold to raise money for charity.

EVERYDAY SUPERHERO

Name: Kurembera

Job: Mountain gorilla

Superpower: I have thick fur to survive on the mountains in Rwanda

How extinction affects you: Due to disease (I can catch human diseases), war and habitat loss

Top tip: Sponsor a mountain gorilla

Hates: Traps set by humans that can kill or injure my friends

Loves: Living peacefully in the cloud forest

KUREMBERA

RAISING FUNDS FOR ANIMALS

Lots of charities all over the world take care of many different types of animals. Through conservation work, by employing local rangers to keep them safe or by doing research to find out how we can best look after them. They all need money to survive and do their work, sadly.

You can make a massive difference to them by organizing fundraisers, doing sponsored events or even baking cakes. It's a great way to make a difference away from home.

YOUR 2 MINUTE MISSION: Get together with your friends and have a superhero meeting and think up fundraising ideas to raise money for animal charities. 15 POINTS

HOW ABOUT SOME OF THESE FUN IDEAS?

♠ Set up the Superhero Car Wash
♠ Bake superhero cakes and sell them
♠ Organize a fancy dress day at school
♠ Hold a jumble sale
♠ Organize a raft race or duck race
♠ Organize a 24 hour dance-off
♠ Hold a skateboard marathon
♠ Play Superhero Bingo

Raising money isn't easy. But it can be done in all kinds of ways. You could ask people to sponsor you, set up a just giving page (www.justgiving.com) or do something as simple as pass around a money box. It also doesn't have to be thousands that you raise. Every penny you raise will help animals in some way. And if it stops one, just one, from going extinct then it's all worth it.

FIGHT EXTINCTION WITH YOUR CLOTHES

How could what you wear possibly have anything to do with fighting extinction? Well, funnily enough, just like lots of other areas of life, what you wear has an effect on the planet, and also on nature.

The best news though, is that you can do something about it.

Fashion uses up huge amounts of energy, takes up land to grow crops, takes up water to wash and make the clothes or uses fossil fuels to make fabrics that do not degrade and which pollute the planet long after they have been worn out.

WHAT ARE YOU WEARING?

You might think of your clothes as just your clothes, right? Of course they are. But every item of clothing you or your parents or carers buys for you has an impact on nature and the planet. Some are worse for the planet than others, and that means they are bad for nature.

FUR AND SKINS

It used to be fashionable to wear animal fur and animal skins. While you won't see many new clothes made from these today, the fashion industry still uses animals to make clothes.

People still wear shoes made out of snakeskin or carry handbags made from crocodiles. They might even wear feathers from birds of paradise or have hats made from beavers. All of them are endangered in some way or other.

HOW "NATURAL" FIBRES CAUSE EXTINCTION

Viscose is a fabric that's made from wood pulp. In some countries forest is cut down and native trees are used in this process. In other places forest is cut down to grow plantations, which is wrecking local biodiversity.

HOW MAN-MADE FIBRES CAUSE EXTINCTION

Man-made fibres are those that are made from fossil fuels. The fashion industry is extremely wasteful, uses up huge amounts of energy and produces huge amounts of carbon dioxide. It also uses a lot of fossil fuels, which themselves produce huge amounts of carbon dioxide. The long and short of it is that fashion – and particularly fast fashion – is bad for the planet and for nature.

HOW DO YOU FIGHT EXTINCTION WITH YOUR CLOTHES?

Well, it's quite simple really. All you have to do is stop buying cheap clothes, clothes made from man-made fibres or clothes that use animals. There are lots of ways to do this and still be bang on trend. Here are some other fashion-friendly ideas to help you fight extinction – you super stylish superhero!

LEARN TO SEW:
Making your own clothes isn't very easy. But learning how to sew will give you an amazing superpower: fixing things!!! It means your favourite clothes will live longer and have a happier life.

SHOP SECOND HAND:
Giving clothes a new life from a charity shop not only helps you to save money, it also helps the charity and helps to reduce the demand for new clothes.

YOUR 2 MINUTE MISSION: **Ask your parents, grandparents or carers to teach you how to sew. Start with sewing on a button, then try something like mending a hole or a patch. 20 POINTS**

YOUR 2 MINUTE MISSION: **Set yourself a ridiculously low budget – say £5 – and go clothes shopping. Get yourself a brand new outfit for a party or even a fancy dress party and save ££££, plus have fun!!! 20 POINTS**

BUY ONCE AND WELL:
Save your pennies and buy something you REALLY love, then wear it until it falls apart! Then mend it!

SWAP YOUR TOGS:
Your old clothes might be useless and unwanted to you but they won't be to other people.

REVAMP YOUR WARDROBE:
Clothes that don't fit or that aren't exciting anymore can be revamped by sewing on patches, changing the buttons or cutting off arms and legs!!!

YOUR 2 MINUTE MISSION: Save your pocket money and then buy yourself something you really like and want. It will help you to fight extinction by not buying lots of cheap stuff. **20 POINTS**

YOUR 2 MINUTE MISSION: Get your classmates to bring in all their unwanted clothes to school. Then swap! **20 POINTS**

MISSION 13
FIGHT EXTINCTION WITH YOUR VOICE

While some people say that actions speak louder than words, some superheroes are great at using their voice to make a protest and, as a result, make things happen. When it comes to extinctions it's important to let the people who can make a difference know how you feel.

If you are brave, people will listen.

It's not easy to stand up and use your voice. But sometimes that's what you have to do. Your teachers are very cool (did you know they are secret superheroes too) and will listen to you if you want to speak in assembly or your class, especially if it's about the welfare of the planet.

You can use your voice in lots of other ways too. Find out how in this chapter.

YOUR 2 MINUTE MISSION:
Write a song, rap or poem.
Many superheroes have used music and poetry to protest over the years.
20 POINTS

START A CAMPAIGN

In 2018 Greta Thunberg decided to strike for climate change. Every Friday she went to the Swedish parliament and sat outside with a placard. Lots of people followed her, and in 2019 climate strikes took place all across the world. From one small action Greta has influenced millions of people around the world to do the same and has been the voice of the young against a terrible threat.

You could do this too. But. Think about what you do carefully. Some adults won't like it if you miss school or disrupt "normal life" by protesting. So talk it through with your parents or carers and teachers and make a protest that will enable you to use your voice and make a point but not upset anyone (except those who need to act).

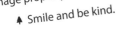

HOW TO BE A SUPERHERO ACTIVIST:

♠ Be nice!!

♠ Make placards and march around your playground.

♠ Set up a stall at a local fair or in your high street.

♠ Be clear about your aims.

♠ Be ready to explain why you are protesting.

♠ Don't damage property or hurt people's feelings.

♠ Smile and be kind.

MAKE A MOVEMENT

I started by doing a #2minutebeachclean every time I went to the beach. Now, some years later, my idea has turned into a charity with lots of people supporting it and almost 1,000 beach cleaning stations around the coast.

YOUR 2 MINUTE MISSION: Start a club or a group to help nature. You could plant trees or recycle rubbish. Celebrate doing good things for the planet. 30 POINTS

JOIN A MARCH

Talk to your family about going on a protest or march against extinction. You can find out times and details online. Tell them why you'd like to go and explain to them why you are worried about extinction, both here and abroad. Make a placard and make sure your voice gets heard!

YOUR 2 MINUTE MISSION: Make a placard. Write a message on it that explains what you are protesting for. Make it funny or emotional and very memorable. 20 POINTS

TIME TO TALK

Talking about extinction is the first step in getting anything done about it. But it is a BIG conversation. Try breaking things down so it's easier for people to understand.

- Tell them what the problems are.
- Smash them with some GREAT facts.
- Tell them what they need to do to help.
- Make sure it's easy and simple.
- Explain what you are asking for.
- Give good reasons why you are asking them to do it.

YOUR 2 MINUTE MISSION: Talk to your friends and family about how to help nature and animals at risk. 50 POINTS

FIGHT EXTINCTION AT SCHOOL

You spend a lot of time at school. In days it adds up to about half of your year. While you have to work hard studying, there is still plenty of time to fight extinction during your break times or in free periods. So why not?

You've already completed a lot of missions at home and in your garden that will help fight extinction. Now is the time to take what you learned into school!

Your teachers, believe it or not, are superheroes too. Many of them will care deeply about nature and the planet and will do their very best to make sure that the planet you inherit is happy and healthy. So please don't be afraid to talk to them. Show them this page and ask that you find some time to talk about extinction and nature.

A MESSAGE FROM ME TO YOUR TEACHER

Dear Teacher,

Thanks for taking the time to read this. Your pupil has been reading this book because they care deeply about the environment and want to do their best to look after nature and the planet. They are, as you already know, on the road to becoming a superhero and I'd love it if you could support them in this. Please listen to their concerns and work with them to make your school, and the planet, a place where nature can thrive.

Thank you,

Martin

⭐ **EVERYDAY SUPERHERO** ⭐

Name: Sir or Miss

Job: Your teacher

Superpower: Making learning fun

How you fight extinction: I teach kids how to love nature and how to look after it

Top tip: Listen to your teacher. Bring them an apple (of a local variety) and thank them for teaching you

Hates: When people don't listen to the concerns of my students

Loves: When kids fight extinction!!!

CARLY

YOUR 2 MINUTE MISSION: Hold an extinction assembly – it's a great time to talk to your schoolmates, even if it's a bit scary. But with the help of your friends, you could make it really fun and interesting for everyone. 20 POINTS

HELP ANIMALS AT SCHOOL

The more you can help your school to reduce the energy you use and the waste you create, the more you fight extinction and help animals and the planet!

SAVE ENERGY

Your school uses energy to power the lights and the computers, and, just like at home, your school also produces waste, such as paper and plastic.

YOUR 2 MINUTE MISSION: **Turn off all the lights and computers at night or when a classroom is empty. Make labels to remind everyone before they leave to go home. 10 POINTS**

PAPER WASTE

Using less paper is a great way to fight extinction as it means less forest is cut down to make it. Forests that are specially grown to make paper are usually lacking in biodiversity – because they contain only one type of tree – and take up land that should be natural forest where nature can thrive.

YOUR 2 MINUTE MISSION: **Save paper – and trees. Try to print out less things and print double-sided to save paper. Write on both sides of a piece of paper and recycle when you're done! 10 POINTS**

PLASTIC WASTE

Plastic is dangerous for wildlife if it gets into the environment. If you use less of it, you'll be helping to fight extinction, because every piece of plastic has an adverse effect on nature.

YOUR 2 MINUTE MISSION: Talk to your teacher and classmates and encourage them to use less plastic at school. 10 POINTS

FOOD WASTE

You can help fight extinction even on your lunch break. Reducing food waste will help save the energy needed to dispose of it at a recycling facility, where it may produce methane, a climate gas, as it breaks down. You can also reduce the use of those pesky single-use plastics that you might find in your lunch box, such as plastic straws and food bags.

YOUR 2 MINUTE MISSION: Save on food waste by eating all of your lunch – yum! If you can't eat it all, ask for smaller portions. 10 POINTS

YOUR 2 MINUTE MISSION: Make your lunches plastic-free by using reusable containers. 10 POINTS

105

JOIN YOUR SCHOOL COUNCIL

I'm sorry to say but it's the grown-ups that are causing extinctions. I don't mean it's your parents or teachers. I mean the people in charge of the planet, such as politicians and corporations, who don't think of nature and the environment first.

How can you change this? Join them. You can start by joining your school council. As a school councillor you will get to have a say in how your school is run. That means you'll be able to make sure that the subject of extinction is talked about and acted upon. After that, set your aims high. We could use a decent Prime Minister. You could do better. Why? Because you are a superhero.

YOUR 2 MINUTE MISSION: Join your school council to help change the rules so you can fight extinction and speak up for nature. If your school doesn't have a council, start one. You have the right to have a say! 50 POINTS

LET NATURE INTO YOUR SCHOOL

Schools are great places for nature to thrive, if you let it. And there are so many things you could do to help your school grounds become a wildlife haven, a refuge for birds and a dinner table for insects. Even if you live in a city there are things you can do to let nature in to your school!

YOUR 2 MINUTE MISSION: **Talk to your teacher and classmates about planning a wildlife area for plants, insects and animals to find a home. 20 POINTS**

Try the ideas below! Some of them might not be right for your school. However, discussing them will help to bring it to the attention of your class and will help to make a difference.

Plant native apple trees and measure them as they grow.

Plan a wildlife pond that will attract frogs, newts and insects.

Grow salad on your classroom windowsills to eat instead of having plastic wrapped lettuce or tomatoes.

Talk to the groundskeeper about leaving part of your school field to grow long so it attracts bees, insects and invertebrates.

FIGHT EXTINCTION WHEN YOU TRAVEL

The average superhero gets about a bit. You travel to school, to the shops and, sometimes, you even get to go on holiday (because superheroes need a break, right?). How you do this, and what you do when you get there, can make a real difference to nature and the natural world.

GOING TO SCHOOL

While you might not think travelling by car has got much to do with extinctions, it's still relevant. Travelling by car, and relying on the car, creates climate gases and pollution which affects the whole planet. And that is one factor that's affecting nature all over the world. So the less you travel by car, the better.

YOUR 2 MINUTE MISSION: **If it's possible to walk to school, try it for one day a week. Could you get together with friends to walk together and create a "walking bus"? Each day you walk instead of riding in the car helps save the planet (and makes you fitter too!) 20 POINTS**

YOUR 2 MINUTE MISSION: **Cycling is another really efficient way of travelling that doesn't harm the planet. If you don't have a Bikeability scheme at your school, talk to your teachers about learning to ride safely. 20 POINTS**

PLANE:

Per passenger, planes give off the most carbon per kilometre. So don't go to school in your private jet. Not even if you have one!

TRAIN:

Trains use less fuel per passenger than cars. Let the train take the strain!

BUS:

Better than travelling by car. Less pollution, traffic and carbon is better for the planet!

CAR:

Cars produce emissions and pollution and use fossil fuels. Not so great for the planet and nature.

WALKING:

Brilliant!!! Just don't tread on any creepy-crawlies!

CYCLING:

Amazing. All you use is your leg power.

GOING ON HOLIDAY

Travelling, whether by car, train or plane, gives out greenhouse gases and contributes to climate change, as we know, and this is having an adverse effect on animals everywhere, endangering them and contributing to extinctions. So, to fight extinction, we must also fight climate change.

Going on holiday can create a lot of climate gases, especially if you go abroad, but, if you do you can do lots to help animals and nature. So the less you travel by car the better.

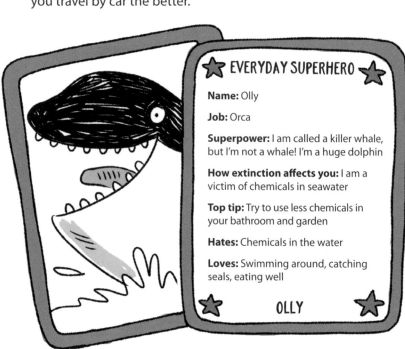

⭐ EVERYDAY SUPERHERO ⭐

Name: Olly

Job: Orca

Superpower: I am called a killer whale, but I'm not a whale! I'm a huge dolphin

How extinction affects you: I am a victim of chemicals in seawater

Top tip: Try to use less chemicals in your bathroom and garden

Hates: Chemicals in the water

Loves: Swimming around, catching seals, eating well

OLLY

THE AMAZING EXTINCTIONCATION

Staycations are holidays you take at home. They are good for extinction and the planet because you create less climate gases from using transport. Pretend you are in a hotel and have big breakfasts before going out to explore nature near you.

> YOUR 2 MINUTE MISSION: Talk to your parents or carers about your next holiday and doing something that's planet positive. 40 POINTS

Visit animal refuges and charities that save animals.

Do a #2minutebeachclean or #2minutelitterpick.

Make it a plastic-free vacation: Take your water bottle, metal straw and reusable bags!

Try eco-friendly activities. (Sorry, no jet skis!)

FIGHT EXTINCTION WITH YOUR PEN

Your last task is about being creative with words and pictures to help the animals. The pen is mightier than the sword, and you have the power to tell the people in charge or the people who make the rules what you would like for them to do. Use your pens and pencils to fight extinction.

YOUR 2 MINUTE MISSION: Draw a poster to put up in school about animals or plants that are in danger near you. Make the poster exciting and visual so that your teachers see it and will be compelled to act. 50 POINTS

Make a home for nature
in our school
NOW!

Dear Prime Minister,

My name is [INSERT YOUR NAME HERE]. I am [YOUR AGE HERE]. I am writing to you because I am worried about extinction, biodiversity loss and the destruction of natural habitats.

I have taken lots of actions in the fight against extinction. [LIST THEM HERE] I have built a bee hotel so that our local bee population can find a home. I have also persuaded my parents to stop mowing our lawn so that insects can find food. I have helped to build a pond for wildlife at my school. I have also spoken to my friends and family about extinctions.

I have done all I can. But I can't make important decisions about how our society treats nature or pass laws that halt the illegal wildlife trade or that encourage rewilding. I can't ban plastic packaging and single-use plastics. I can't control the use of pesticides and bee-killing chemicals. I can't designate marine protection zones or stop destructive road or rail building projects. I can't talk to foreign leaders and agree on the protection of animals and nature.

But you can. While you might not feel the full effects of climate change and extinctions in your lifetime, I will. That's why I'd like you to pledge to do more to protect nature and the environment in order to avoid this global crisis.

Yours [SIGN HERE]

MISSION COMPLETED

Now you have completed your missions it's time to look back at what you have achieved and what effect it may have had. Firstly though, I'd like to thank you for all the work you have done, on behalf of nature. It means your future could be in a world that is full of nature, wonder and biodiversity, on a healthy planet where humans and nature live happily side by side. How wonderful!

Imagine yourself, in harmony with the planet, riding your bike, eating great food, loving life and having fun. The skies are full of birds, the meadows are full of flowers and buzzing with insects and bees and the rivers are clear and cool and full of fish.

You helped to do that!!!

You've talked to friends and family about the crisis in nature to raise awareness.

You've saved up to sponsor an animal at your local zoo or donated a bit of your pocket money to conservation charities. You might even have done a sponsored skateboard for them too. Go dude!!!

You've grown a meadow in your garden for bees and insects by persuading your parents to stop mowing.

You've planted a tree that will become a home for thousands of tiny creatures, birds and insects.

You've given bees the food and homes they deserve so they can pollinate our crops.

You've found out what's in your food and what a difference it makes to the planet to avoid some ingredients. Hopefully you've said goodbye to palm oil FOR EVER!

You've had a hit record (well, nearly) and you've written to the Prime Minister. That's a BIG DEAL.

It all adds up to make a difference, and when you add it to all the work that the other superheroes have done it's MASSIVE. So let's keep spreading the word. Let's not stop until we've made a difference and nature is restored.

You will be able to find your superhero rating on the following pages but for now, let's raise a cheer to you THE SUPERHERO for helping to save nature and carry the message far and wide.

You are my hero.
Thank you,
Martin

YOUR SUPERHERO RATING...

SUPERHERO POINTS

Now that you've finished your training, it's time to discover what kind of superhero you are. Add up the points you've earned by completing your missions.

MISSION 1: GET TO KNOW EXTINCTION

Use your superhero eyes to go on a fossil hunt! **10 POINTS**

Go to the park, the countryside or even just your garden. Sit quietly for a couple of minutes and see if you can spot a dinosaur. (CLUE: Birds are distant relatives of dinosaurs.)
5 POINTS

TOTAL MISSION POINTS: 15

MISSION 3: THE PLANET IN BALANCE

Make a terrarium. It is a self-sustaining ecosystem. It's pretty easy to make one although you might need some help from an adult. **15 POINTS**

Draw your own food chain.
It could be real or imagined, and get to understand the link between one animal and the next. What will eat what? Are they dinosaurs? Elephants? Sharks? Dolphins? GO WILD!
5 POINTS

TOTAL MISSION POINTS: 20

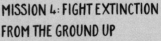

MISSION 4: FIGHT EXTINCTION FROM THE GROUND UP

Go outside and see if you can find any creepy-crawlies. Don't get too close or touch them, especially if you are afraid of them. Replace any stones carefully and try not to harm any of them. **10 POINTS**

Get to know your creepy-crawlies better. Books can help you identify insects. Apps are great at helping you find out what they do and how they act. (Beware: some may have in-app purchases). **5 POINTS**

Weedkiller is terrible for insects and invertebrates. Ask your parents, school and local council to stop using it, if they do. You can write letters and emails or even start a protest. **10 POINTS**

Name your pet spider. Spiders are great. So, next time you find one, don't harm it. Give it a name, let it do its stuff and be its friend. **10 POINTS**

Inspire your friends to take care of insects too. Could you dress up like an insect? Or maybe you could write a story about your pet spider?
10 POINTS

TOTAL MISSION POINTS: 45

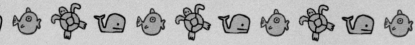

MISSION 5: FIGHT EXTINCTION IN THE GARDEN

Can you see plants growing in the cracks in the pavement, in gaps in walls and in spaces that are unloved or forgotten? Isn't it amazing how nature always seems to find a way to grow – no matter how hard we make it! **5 POINTS**

Take this book outside and see if you can spot any invasive species. If it's Japanese knotweed you'll need to tell an adult. It is a controlled substance and allowing it to spread can result in big fines! **10 POINTS**

Download a plant identification app. Then go out into the garden or park and try to identify a few plants. Are they considered weeds? Are they friend or foe? You decide, based on how you think they help the natural world. **10 POINTS**

In the autumn, plant a bee-friendly flower pot with bulbs of crocus, snowdrop, grape hyacinth and scented daffodil. The bulbs will produce flowers in spring when the bees need them most. **30 POINTS**

Make a bee hotel. **50 POINTS**

Let dandelions grow in your garden. Dandelions are among the first flowers to bloom in spring. That means bees can get a jolly good feast on nectar soon after a long winter or hibernation. **10 POINTS**

Talk to the mower in your family about mowing every three weeks, instead of every week. **10 POINTS**

Want to earn some pocket money and help save the planet? Offer to mow the lawn! If you raise the height of the cutting blades to their maximum (get some help with this) it will help insects and birds. **20 POINTS**

Make a flyer to put in the letterboxes in your street asking people to cut down their mowing from once a week to once every three weeks. Make it colourful and don't forget to include facts from this book. **10 POINTS**

TOTAL MISSION POINTS: 155

MISSION 6: FIGHT EXTINCTION AT THE BIRD TABLE

Make a birdy cake for the birds to eat! It's really easy (but you might need to get a little help from one of your pet adults). **30 POINTS**

Make a bird cafe. It can be as simple as hanging birdy cakes off a hook on your balcony. But if you have help and a few bits of wood, it's easy. **50 POINTS**

Take a book out of the library or download an app and learn to identify the birds that visit your bird cafe. **10 POINTS**

TOTAL MISSION POINTS: 90

MISSION 7: FIGHT EXTINCTION WITH WATER

Harvesting rainwater is really easy to do. Put out a bucket on your windowsill, balcony or in the garden and see how much water you collect when it rains. Save it and use it to water your plants, either indoors or outdoors, when they need it.
10 POINTS

Speak to your parents or carers about setting up a water barrel. If you grow plants it will be useful to water them with. **10 POINTS**

Make a simple washing up bowl pond. **10 POINTS**

TOTAL MISSION POINTS: 30

MISSION 8: FIGHT EXTINCTION AT THE SUPERMARKET

Find a food that your family eats regularly. Check out the ingredients. If it's GM or has palm oil in it, find an alternative, if you can. Do a price comparison. Is it cheaper or more expensive? **10 POINTS**

Add organic material such as compost to your garden. Worms are the heroes of the mud. They recycle dead matter – like leaves and dead flowers – and turn it into healthy, nutrient-rich soil that's great for growing. **20 POINTS**

While you might not be able to change what your family buys, you can look at the labels on the food they buy. Check it out. See where it comes from. Take a look at some of the ingredients they use. **10 POINTS**

Check out the labels of foods you suspect may have soya. It may be difficult. But if it says it's from Brazil, avoid it. **10 POINTS**

Look at the labels on your shopping. See if you can spot the palm oil.
10 POINTS

TOTAL MISSION POINTS: 60

MISSION 9: FIGHT EXTINCTION IN THE KITCHEN

Apples are grown all over the world. But here in the UK there are a few varieties that are native. See if you can find them in your local shops.
10 POINTS

Look at your favourite fish dish and then go and look at www.mcsuk. org/goodfishguide to see how your fish fared on the Good Fish Guide. Did it do OK? Great!!! Not so good??

Maybe it's time to change brand or try something different. **20 POINTS**

Go vegan for a day. I bet you'll find that you'll get to love being a plant-based superhero. If you like it, why not go vegan one day each week? **50 POINTS**

Make oat milk and try it on your cereal. It's the very best milk for the planet. **40 POINTS**

TOTAL MISSION POINTS: 120

MISSION 10: FIGHT EXTINCTION IN THE BATHROOM

Check out your bathroom products and work out which ones are planet-friendly and which ones are not. Look for palm oil, plastic, nasty chemicals and unsustainable ingredients. See if you can spot the RSPO logo on any product. **10 POINTS**

Visit a waste-free shop. They have lots of products that are plastic-free and good for the planet. Look for soap that's doesn't contain palm oil and shampoo bars that you can rub on your head! **20 POINTS**

Done your missions? Good. Now it's time to have some superhero fun. Relax with an eco-friendly, home-made, luxury bath bomb. **50 POINTS**

TOTAL MISSION POINTS: 80

MISSION 11: FIGHT EXTINCTION WITH YOUR POCKET MONEY

Find an empty glass jar and a sticker. Write FOR FIGHTING EXTINCTION on the sticker and then stick it on the jar. Every time you have change, put it in the jar. When the jar is full, empty it and donate it to charity. **30 POINTS**

You could use your pocket money to adopt an animal. Work out how much you can save each week and then put it in your EXTINCTION BANK to use later to adopt your favourite animal. **20 POINTS**

Get together with your friends and have a superhero meeting and think up fundraising ideas to raise money for animal charities. **15 POINTS**

TOTAL MISSION POINTS: 65

MISSION 12: FIGHT EXTINCTION WITH YOUR CLOTHES

Ask your parents, grandparents or carers to teach you how to sew. Start with sewing on a button, then try something like mending a hole or a patch. **20 POINTS**

Set yourself a ridiculously low budget – say £5 – and go clothes shopping. Get yourself a brand new outfit for a party or even a fancy dress party and save ££££,

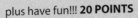

plus have fun!!! **20 POINTS**

Save your pocket money and then buy yourself something you really like and want. It will help you to fight extinction by not buying lots of cheap stuff. **20 POINTS**

Get your classmates to bring in all their unwanted clothes to school. Then swap! **20 POINTS**

TOTAL MISSION POINTS: 80

MISSION 13: FIGHT EXTINCTION WITH YOUR VOICE

Write a song, rap or poem. Many superheroes have used music and poetry to protest over the years. **20 POINTS**

Start a club or a group to help nature. You could plant trees or recycle rubbish. Celebrate doing good things for the planet. **30 POINTS**

Make a placard. Write a message on it that explains what you are protesting for. Make it funny or emotional and very memorable. **20 POINTS**

Talk to your friends and family about how to help nature and animals at risk. **50 POINTS**

TOTAL MISSION POINTS: 120

MISSION 14: FIGHT EXTINCTION AT SCHOOL

Hold an extinction assembly – it's a great time to talk to your schoolmates, even if it's a bit scary. But with the help of your friends, you could make it really fun and interesting for everyone. **20 POINTS**

Turn off all the lights and computers at night or when a classroom is empty. Make labels to remind everyone before they leave to go home. **10 POINTS**

Save paper – and trees. Try to print out less things and print double-sided to save paper. Write on both sides of a piece of paper and recycle when you're done! **10 POINTS**

Talk to your teacher and classmates and encourage them to use less plastic at school. **10 POINTS**

Save on food waste by eating all of your lunch – yum! If you can't eat it all, ask for smaller portions. **10 POINTS**

Make your lunches plastic-free by using reusable containers. **10 POINTS**

Join your school council to help change the rules so you can fight extinction and speak up for nature. If your school doesn't have a council,

start one. You have the right to have a say! **50 POINTS**

Talk to your teacher and classmates about planning a wildlife area for plants, insects and animals to find a home. **20 POINTS**

TOTAL MISSION POINTS: 140

MISSION 15: FIGHT EXTINCTION WHEN YOU TRAVEL

If it's possible to walk to school, try it for one day a week. Could you get together with friends to walk together and create a "walking bus"? Each day you walk instead of riding in the car helps save the planet (and makes you fitter too!) **20 POINTS**

Cycling is another really efficient way of travelling that doesn't harm the planet. If you don't have a Bikeability scheme at your school, talk to your teachers about learning to ride safely. **20 POINTS**

Talk to your parents or carers about your next holiday and doing something that's planet positive. **40 POINTS**

TOTAL MISSION POINTS: 80

BONUS MISSION: FIGHT EXTINCTION WITH YOUR PEN

Draw a poster to put up in school about animals or plants that are in danger near you. Make the poster exciting and visual so that your teachers see it and will be compelled to act. **50 POINTS**

Write a letter to someone important who can act on a global scale. You can use this template to write to the Prime Minister of the UK, but it could be your MP or local councillor. **100 POINTS**

TOTAL MISSION POINTS: 150

WHAT KIND OF SUPERHERO ARE YOU?

Now you have completed the tasks, take a look at what kind of superhero you are. How did you do? Well, actually, can I let you into a secret? It doesn't really matter. The most important thing is that you do something, anything to fight extinction.

You are a-maz-ing.

0-499 POINTS

Fantastic! You have done so well to come this far you little superhero in the making. I applaud your commitment and urge you to keep going! With just a few more tasks under your belt you'll be well on the road to Gold Star Superhero status. Mind you, the work you have done to date will add up to make a difference, and that's what matters. Go you. Go nature. We are winning!!!

MISSION COMPLETE: You're a Grade 1 Superhero!

500-999 POINTS

Hey there. You are doing an awesome job. Stardust awaits you. From doing a few simple things to help nature you have shown true commitment. I am so glad to have you on our team. With your help the natural world is having a boost.

MISSION COMPLETE: You're a real Grade 2 Superhero!

OVER 1,000 POINTS

You rock. Thanks to your work – and your work talking to others – you are making a difference. You are a true, top notch superhero and I am proud to know you. You aren't just on the team, you are leading from the front and setting the very best example. Brilliant work.

MISSION COMPLETE: You win the Grade 3 Superhero Award!

INSERT YOUR PHOTO HERE

EVERYDAY SUPERHERO

What's your name?

What's your job?

What's your superpower?

How do you fight extinction?

What's your top tip?

What do you hate?

What do you love?

YOU

FIND OUT MORE ABOUT THE FIGHT AGAINST EXTINCTION

Want to find out how to get involved? Great! Take a look at these:

CAMPAIGNS AND ACTIVISM

The World Wildlife Fund: a charity with lots of information and online resources for superheroes

www.wwf.org.uk/get-involved/schools/resources

People's Trust for Endangered Species: a charity set up to help wildlife in the UK and worldwide

www.ptes.org

International Union for Conservation of Nature: an international organization that monitors species to help protect nature

www.iucn.org

Extinction Rebellion: look for family events and local family groups

www.extinctionrebellion.uk

RESOURCES

Royal Society for the Prevention of Cruelty to Animals: the RSPCA have free educational resources available online

www.education.rspca.org.uk

MORE ABOUT MARTIN

Hello. I am Martin Dorey. I'm a surfer, writer, beach lover and anti-plastic and climate change activist. I live near the sea in Cornwall with my partner, Lizzy, who is also known as Dr Seaweed. She's a gardener and botanist and helps me to understand plants and photosynthesis and all that exciting stuff! My children, Maggie and Charlotte, live down the road from me with their dog Bob. Maggie is a lifeguard and Charlotte makes a lot of her own clothes. I like surfing, walking, being outside and trying to grow vegetables. I also cook a lot, especially when I'm in my camper van. I also like my bike, cleaning beaches and waking up to sunny days by the sea with the people I love the most.

MORE ABOUT THE #2MINUTEFOUNDATION

The 2 Minute Foundation (www.2minute.org) is a charity that is devoted to cleaning up the planet 2 minutes at a time. The idea is very simple: each time you go to the beach, the park or anywhere at all, use 2 minutes to pick up litter, take a picture of it and then post it to social media to inspire others to do the same.

In 2014, we set up a network of 8 Beach Clean Stations around Cornwall that make it easy for people to pick up litter at the beach. Now, in 2022, we have over 1,000 of them! Some are even made from the plastic we picked up off the beach! We have thousands of followers who help the planet every day by cleaning beaches, cutting out plastic from their lives or picking up litter from the streets where they live.

With thanks to:
Lizzy, my semi-tame botanist (and best mate);
Tim Wesson;
Daisy, Charlie, Laurissa, Faith and all at Walker Books;
Tim Bates at Peters Fraser and Dunlop Literary Agents;
the **2 Minute Foundation** family;
Chris Hines;
and anyone else who has made an effort, no matter how small,
to make a difference.